My Little Book of
Animals

by Camilla de la Bédoyère

Sandy Creek
NEW YORK

Sandy Creek
NEW YORK

An Imprint of Sterling Publishing
387 Park Avenue South
New York, NY 10016

ISBN 978-1-4351-5526-8

Manufactured in Guangdong, China
Lot #:
2 4 6 8 10 9 7 5 3 1
04/14

Words in **bold**
are explained in
the glossary on
page 60.

Contents

Lions

Lions live in Africa where
they hunt for their food.

⩔ **This lioness looks scary,
but she is yawning! Lions
like to sleep a lot.**

>> **A male lion has
thick hair around his
head called a mane.**

These cats are big, strong, and fierce. They live in groups, called prides. Each pride is ruled by a male lion.

⌃ A lioness looks after her cubs, and will teach them how to hunt.

Elephants

Elephants are the biggest animals that live on land. They have enormous ears and long trunks.

∧ Baby elephants love to play.

▼ **This family of African elephants is drinking at a** waterhole.

An elephant's trunk is a nose, but it works like a hand. Elephants can use their trunk to pick a flower, or to lift a branch.

▲ **An Asian elephant cools off with a shower of water!**

Giraffes

Giraffes walk slowly in the hot African sun. They look for tasty leaves to eat from the trees.

>> A giraffe has a long neck and long legs. It is about 16 feet tall when fully grown.

<< It is difficult for giraffes to drink.

A giraffe's fur is gold and brown, like dry grass. This helps it to hide from lions.

⌄ **A giraffe's tongue is almost as long as your arm.**

9

Zebras

Zebras are part of the horse family. They live in large herds on the **grasslands** of Africa.

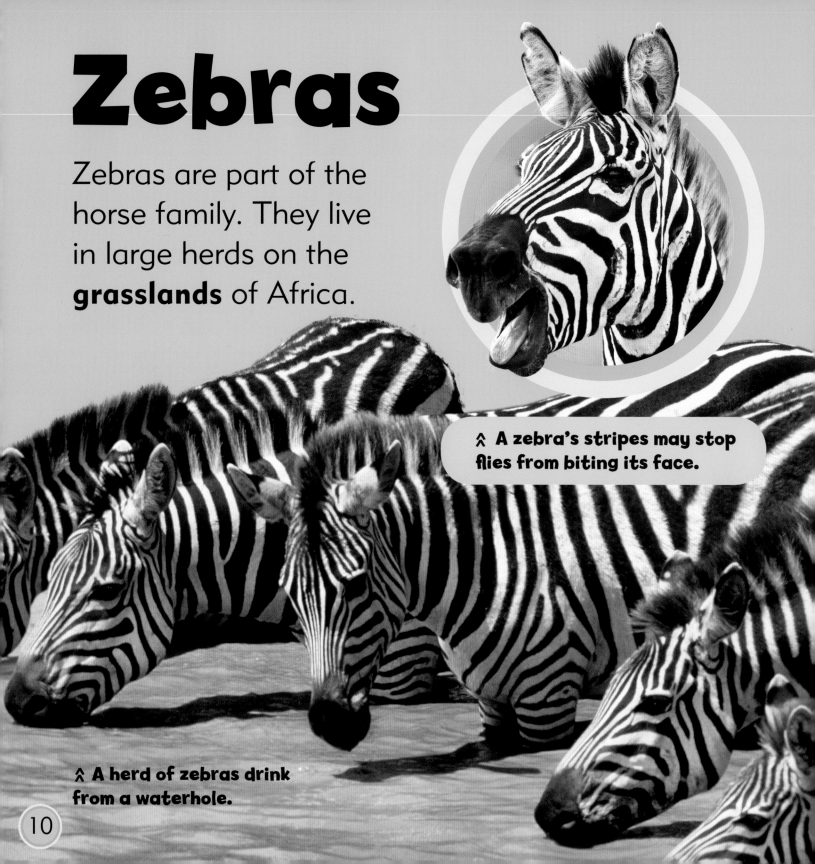

∧ A zebra's stripes may stop flies from biting its face.

∧ A herd of zebras drink from a waterhole.

10

A zebra's eyes are on the sides of its head, so it can see all around. It is always on the lookout for animals that may want to attack.

∧ **Zebras have hooves, and even the** foals **can run fast.**

Kangaroos

Kangaroos live in Australia. They are **marsupials**, which means they care for their babies in a pouch.

« Sometimes male kangaroos fight. They push, kick, and box!

⌵ A kangaroo can jump 33 feet in one bound.

⌵ A baby kangaroo is called a joey. It stays in its mother's pouch.

A kangaroo cannot run, but it can jump using its strong back legs. They eat grass at night, when it is cooler.

Bluebirds

Bluebirds love to sing. Male bluebirds sing as they fly through the trees.

⌄ **Like many birds, bluebirds eat bugs and grubs. They eat fruit, too.**

⌃ **This is a female bluebird. She has a gray head.**

Male bluebirds have blue feathers on their heads and backs, and reddish chests.

⌄ Bluebirds lay their eggs in a nest. Both parents look after the chicks.

Dolphins

Dolphins are very clever **mammals**. They live underwater, but they must come to the surface to breathe.

>> Dolphins are just the right shape for swimming fast underwater.

⌃ Dolphins often leap out of the water, especially when they are swimming in a group.

>> A dolphin can have more than 50 teeth. All the teeth are the same shape.

Groups of dolphins often swim together. They hunt fish by chasing them through the blue water.

17

Orcas

Orcas are also known as killer whales. They live in groups, called pods.

>> Orcas leap out of the water to look for seals to hunt.

⌄ These whales have black backs, white bellies, and white patches near their eyes.

Orcas live in all of the oceans. They hunt seals, turtles, fish, sharks, and birds.

⩢ **Orcas hunt for seals in shallow water.**

Whale Sharks

The whale shark is the biggest fish in the world. It swims slowly through the ocean.

>> A whale shark is about 39 feet long.

Most sharks hunt other animals, but whale sharks are gentle animals. They feed on tiny animals that float in the ocean.

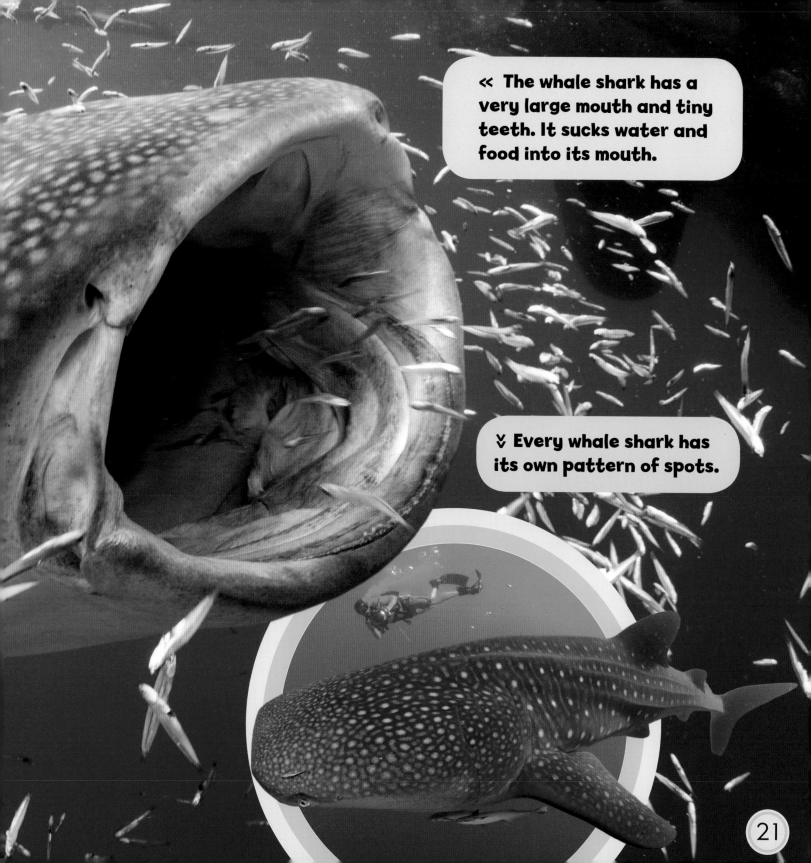

« The whale shark has a very large mouth and tiny teeth. It sucks water and food into its mouth.

∨ Every whale shark has its own pattern of spots.

Angelfish

Many beautiful fish live around **coral reefs**. Some of the most colorful are angelfish.

ˇ Angelfish feed on tiny plants or small sea animals. At night, they hide in coral.

ˇ Some angelfish get more colorful as they get older.

>> These fish have thin bodies.

Hermit Crabs

This odd-looking animal is a hermit crab. It lives in shallow water, around shores and coral reefs.

↑ **Many crabs have eyes on stalks.**

Hermit crabs live inside shells left by other animals. They have two claws, and four walking legs. They also have four more legs hidden in the shell.

« Hermit crabs hide in colorful coral.

∧ When a hermit crab grows too big for its shell, it must move into a bigger one.

Camels

This mammal lives in
the deserts of Africa
and Asia.

« Camels
need long
eyelashes to
keep desert
sand out of
their eyes.

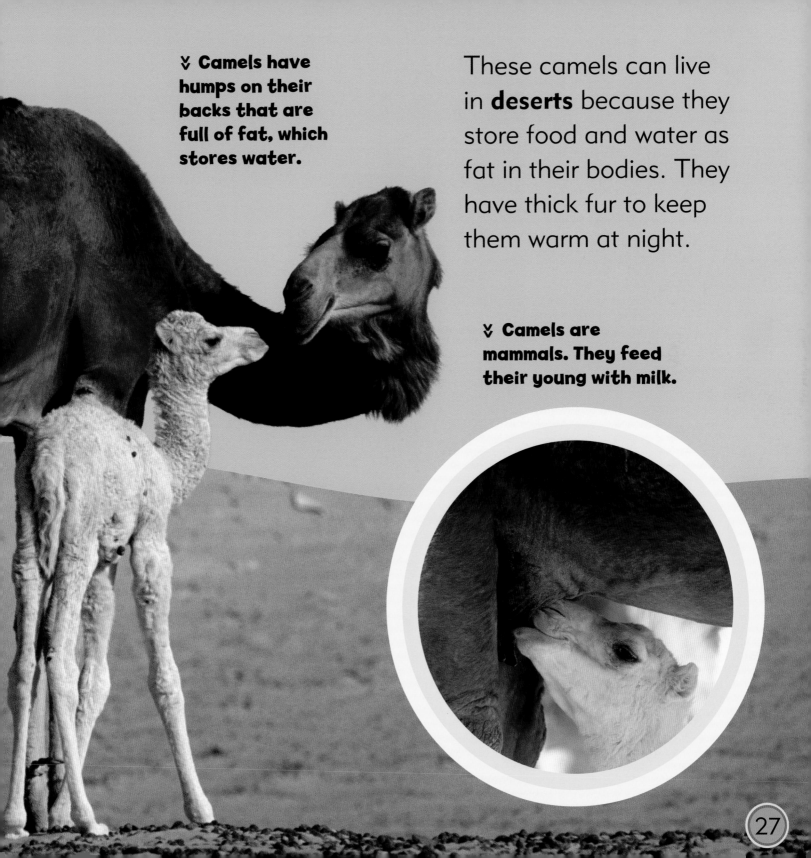

∨ Camels have humps on their backs that are full of fat, which stores water.

These camels can live in **deserts** because they store food and water as fat in their bodies. They have thick fur to keep them warm at night.

∨ Camels are mammals. They feed their young with milk.

Gerbils

This is a gerbil. It is a type of **rodent** that lives in hot, dry places.

⌄ Gerbils often look for food in the early morning, before it gets too hot.

Gerbils are busy little animals that scurry around looking for seeds to eat. They store extra seeds in their **burrows**.

˅ Gerbils hold food in their paws, and nibble at it with their strong teeth.

« A gerbil must watch out for danger.

Ostriches

Ostriches are the largest birds in the world. They live in African deserts.

⌄ **Ostriches use their big eyes to look out for danger.**

^ **Male ostriches look after the eggs and keep them warm!**

<< **Male ostriches have black and white feathers.**

Ostriches must travel far every day to find enough food to eat. They get water from the plants they eat.

Tortoises

Tortoises are **reptiles**. They mostly live in warm places. They have hard shells, and lay eggs.

⌄ Tortoises have small heads, but strong, scaly legs.

« A baby tortoise grows inside its egg for three to five months, until it is ready to hatch.

Tortoises sometimes sleep through very hot or cold times, when it might be too hard to find food.

⌃ This lion cub is prodding a tortoise. The tortoise is safe because it has a hard shell.

Milksnakes

This colorful animal is a milksnake. It is a type of reptile. It has scaly skin, and it lays eggs.

⋁ **This baby snake is just hatching from its egg.**

Most milksnakes are colored red, black, and yellow. They slither around at night looking for bugs, frogs, and small rodents to eat.

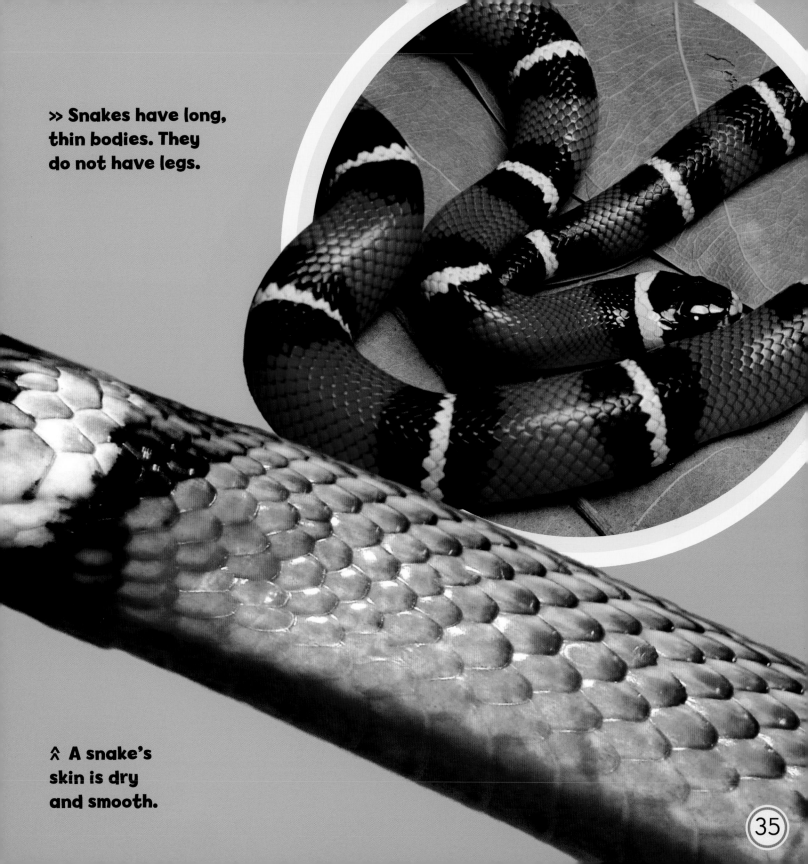

>> Snakes have long, thin bodies. They do not have legs.

⌃ A snake's skin is dry and smooth.

Squirrel Monkeys

This is a squirrel monkey. It lives in a South American **rainforest**, where there is sun and rain most days.

« Monkeys use their hands to grip fruit, nuts, and branches.

« Mother squirrel monkeys look after their babies and teach them how to find food.

A group of monkeys is called a troop. There are often 50 monkeys in a troop. The monkeys work together to find fruit, seeds, and bugs to eat.

∧ Squirrel monkeys can run and leap through the trees.

Panda Bears

This black and white bear is called a panda. It lives in cool mountain forests, in China.

˅ **Panda bears sleep during the day. They curl up in a tree or on a bed of** bamboo.

˄ **Panda bear cubs like to play in the snow.**

« Panda bears need very thick fur to keep them warm.

Panda bears mostly eat bamboo. They eat the shoots, leaves, and stems. Sometimes they eat grubs, too.

Kingfishers

Kingfishers live in forests, and hunt for food in rivers. They are swift, silent hunters.

Kingfishers perch on branches and look for fish in the water below. Then they swoop down and grab the fish.

« This tiny chick has been brought a fish to eat. After four weeks, it will leave the nest.

>> Kingfishers have glossy, blue feathers. They are shy birds.

<< This kingfisher has just caught a slippery fish with its long beak.

41

Chameleons

This colorful animal is a chameleon. It is a type of lizard, and it has dry, scaly skin.

⌄ A chameleon has a long, sticky tongue. It shoots its tongue out to grab tasty bugs to eat.

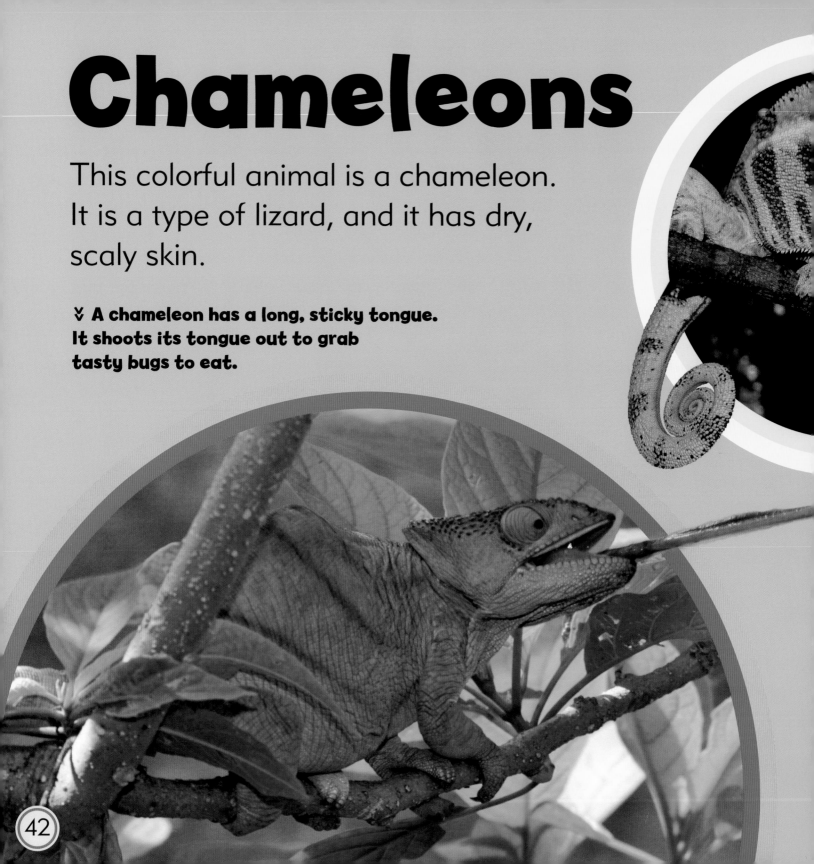

« Some chameleons can change the color of their skin.

» Chameleons can move each eye in a different direction.

Chameleons live in trees. Their green skin helps them to hide among the leaves. They have long tails that they can wrap tightly around branches.

43

Treefrogs

Red-eyed treefrogs are very small. Females are about 3 inches long, and males are even smaller.

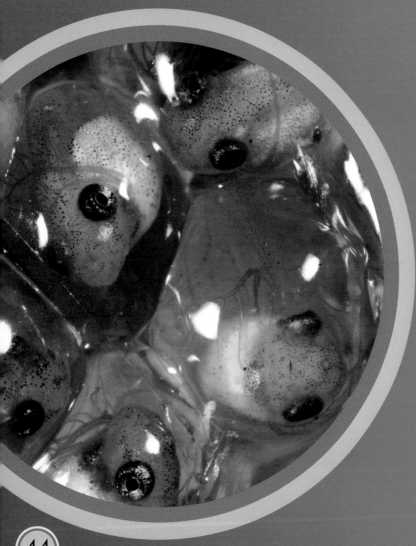

« Treefrogs lay their eggs in trees above water. When they hatch, the tadpoles **fall into the water.**

Frogs are **amphibians**. This means they lay their eggs in, or near, water, and have moist skin. Treefrogs can swim, climb trees, and jump.

^ It takes a few months for treefrog tadpoles to grow into little froglets.

^ Treefrogs live in rainforests, where the air is damp and there are lots of bugs to eat.

Koalas

Koalas are marsupials. They live in **gum trees**, and eat the leaves at night. Koalas stay in the trees for most of their lives.

« When they are not eating, koalas like to sleep.

Koala babies are tiny when they are born. They climb into their mother's pouch and stay there for six months. There, they feed on their mother's milk, and grow bigger.

« **Koalas climb high looking for juicy leaves to eat.**

« **Koalas have two 'thumbs' on their front paws, for gripping tight.**

Tarantulas

Some spiders make nests to catch flies—but not tarantulas. They hunt bigger animals!

« If a tarantula is scared, it flicks hairs at its attacker.

∨ This tarantula is a Mexican red-knee spider. It is one of the biggest spiders in the world.

Tarantula spiders hide in a burrow until it is time to hunt. They are big enough to hunt birds, lizards, and mice. Most spiders kill bugs or other animals with **venom**.

∨ Tarantula spiders are bigger than a grown-up's hand!

Polar Bears

Polar bears are the largest bears of all. They live in very cold places, near the **North Pole**. Their fur is white. This helps them to hide in snowy places.

⌄ When polar bears fight, they use their teeth, paws, and claws.

» A polar bear mother looks after her cubs.

>> Polar bears love to swim. They keep their eyes open underwater.

During the winter, polar bears hunt seals. In the summer, they also eat eggs, small animals, and some plants.

Gray Wolves

Wolves are members of the dog family. They are clever animals that live in family groups, called packs.

⌄ **Gray wolves live in cold forests and mountains.**

⌃ **Wolf cubs are born in the spring. They stay in, or near, their den until they can look after themselves.**

The wolves in a pack hunt together. They chase big animals, such as moose, deer, and **caribou**.

« Wolves are noisy animals. They often howl to tell each other things. Sometimes, the whole pack will howl at once!

Arctic Hares

Arctic hares are able to live in cold places, where there is not much food. They eat plants, but can eat dead animals and other small creatures if they are very hungry.

» Sometimes Arctic hares fight. They box and scratch each other.

« In winter, an Arctic hare has a thick, white winter coat.

In winter, they can be hard to spot against the white snow. This is called **camouflage**.

>> This young hare is losing its winter coat. Its summer coat of brown fur is growing underneath.

Snow Monkeys

Snow monkeys are also known as Japanese macaques. They live in places that get very cold in winter.

« On a cold day, the monkeys huddle together to keep warm.

≪ Snow monkeys have thick fur to keep them warm.

The monkeys like to bathe in hot water pools. The pools are hot because there are **volcanoes** nearby.

⌃ Baby snow monkeys like to play with snow. They make snowballs!

Penguins

King penguins live in the coldest place in the world—the Antarctic. This is the frozen land around the **South Pole**.

« A penguin's body is just the right shape for diving and swimming underwater.

Penguins are birds, but they cannot fly. They swim fast instead. They use their wings like flippers as they swim through the cold Antarctic water, hunting fish to eat.

⌃ King penguins live in colonies. There may be thousands of birds in one colony.

>> This fluffy baby penguin is almost as big as its mother.

Glossary

amphibians A group of animals with soft, moist skin.

bamboo A type of grass that can grow as tall as trees.

burrows Holes or tunnels that small animals dig and use as a home.

camouflage Colors and patterns on an animal that make it hard to spot against its background.

caribou Large deer, also known as reindeer.

coral reefs Stony places built by tiny animals that live in warm seas.

den An animal's home.

deserts Places that get very little rain, or no rain at all.

foals Baby horses or zebras.

froglets Tiny frogs that started life as tadpoles.

grasslands Large areas of land where the main plants that grow are grasses.

grubs The wriggly, wormlike young of some beetles and other insects.

gum tree A type of tree that makes sticky gum in its bark.

hatch To break out of an egg.

hooves The hard part of a horse or zebra's foot.

mammals Animals with fur or hair that feed their young with milk.

marsupials Animals that give birth to tiny babies, which feed and grow in their mother's pouch.

North Pole The place at the top of the world.

rainforest A warm forest where it rains every day.

reptiles Animals with scaly skin. Most reptiles lay eggs.

rodent A small, furry animal with strong teeth that never stop growing.

South Pole The place at the bottom of the world.

tadpoles Baby frogs that live in water.

venom A type of poison.

volcanoes Mountains that sometimes pour out lava (soft, hot rock).

waterhole A pool or pond where wild animals gather to drink.

Index